Embracing The Light In The Dark

Janice Guy

BookLeaf Publishing

India | USA | UK

Presentation by *BookLeaf Publishing*

Web: www.bookleafpub.com

E-mail: info@bookleafpub.com

ISBN:9789358314373

First edition 2023

DEDICATION

To my family, but most of all to my mother who has always encouraged my talents. I love all of you always and in all ways.

ACKNOWLEDGEMENT

I must thank my mother Judith for instilling in me the love of reading and always encouraging me to share my own written word. To my loving husband Tim who brought me out of the darkness and showed me how beautiful my light is. To my children, Hayley, Shaun and Adrian, you three will never know how much your love and light have saved me and continues to do so. To my granddaughter Rowyn and any future grandchildren to come, you fill my heart and soul in ways I have never dreamed of with your infinite love, laughter and joy. Finally, thank you to BookLeaf Publishing, I am positive that it was no accident that I found this writing challenge in the wee hours of the morning. This has ignited a passion in me that has sat dormant in the dark awaiting your light.

PREFACE

This book of poetry, 'Embracing The Light In The Dark', is meant to take the reader on a journey through the resilient human spirit. It is meant to acknowledge that we cannot exist on this earthly plane without acknowledging the good and the bad, the dark and the light and that we must also recognize that not only do both happen to us externally but both exist within us as well.

T.R.A.U.M.A

T-orturous triggers that steal my sense of joy.
         Trauma
R-egressing back to behaviours I thought I had
   overcome.
         Traumas
A-badonment is an ever present battle
   between longing and loneliness.
         Traumatic
U-nrecognizable is the person in the mirror.
         Traumatizing
M-emories flood my mind, relentless as a drug.
         Traumatized
A-larmed is forever my new state of being.
         TRAUMA

Time Does Not Stop

Time must move along,
Regardless of the painstaking moments,
The ones where your knees hit the floor
And the only sound
That echoes from your body,
Is gluttoral.
Time still does not stop.

Time must move along,
Regardless of the intensity
Of unrelenting love.
Staring at the face
Of the one whom you created.
Watching, teaching, learning
And loving as they grow.
Fearing those last moments,
Without knowing when they will be.
Last time you carry them,
Last time you sleep beside them,
Last story read, last lullaby sung.
Every Fiber of your being
Wants to hold on to those moments.
Yet time still does not stop.

Time must move along,
Regardless of being stuck,
In a moment, in a cycle, inside yourself.
It's the one thing we cannot affect.
We try to turn it back.
Physically, spiritually, financially
In our minds and souls.
All things in forward perpetual motion,
Regardless of how far back you are reeling.
When you look around you,
It's hard to believe that the world,
Despite yourself is still spinning.
Time still does not stop.

And yet we stand so still.

Time must move along,
Regardless of our final hours,
Our final moments,
Our final breath.
When the world as we know it
And ourselves in it, cease to exist
Even when we transition
Into eternity as promised.
Time still does not stop.

Universal Story

Life has changed you
Created deep within earth's womb
You have been growing, changing
Forming yourself
With the collection of elements
Along the way
You attach yourself to things
In order to broaden your spectrum
These things alter your state of being
Some things make you shine
while others dull your surface
Some days are rough
Some days are smooth
Your shape and color ever changing

Obvious, to the eye of the beholder
If they would only take notice
No one is the same as another
All uniquely and perfectly created
In your own way
A harrowing journey
You have been on
To become what you are today
If your story was ever told
It would be one of great pressure

Adversity, beauty, triumph and defeat
And here you are,
with poise and strength
Still standing
Strong as Ever
Ready for the next challenge
I want you to know I see you
In all God's glory
I always stop to look around
Even if you seem invisible to the world
You were perfectly planned
An integral part of life on earth
It's strange how closely
The human spirit relates
To the story of a Rock

(To be read both top to bottom and/or bottom to top.)

Rejection Reflection

Chemical peels,
  bleach,
    burns,
      scars,
        and tattoos
      could all change what I can't unsee.

How do I make it so it's not his face looking
    back in the mirror,
      maybe then I can truly love me?

I Surrender

I release the heart racing surge of expectation.
I let go of the tension, of breathing in control.
I cast away the shadow of fear that lurks in my
mind.
Rather,
I embrace being a wide open field
on a breezy summer day.
I ride the rushing wave
carrying the tide out to sea.
I enchantingly free fall
towards an endless universal state of faith.
I surrender fully and completely.
I trust, I love, I believe.
I surrender unto you.

The Box

I stared at that box for hours,
Trying to PrEtZeL myself to fit
Exactly who you needed,
Or maybe who you wanted.
I twisted, turned and contorted
The very essence of myself
Until I squeezed every ounce
Of who I was out, to fit your box.
Only to find another one,
Awaiting my next MeTaMoRpHoSiS.

The Sadist Within

Battered, bruised and beat
Torn down and destroyed
I claim defeat.
All for your pleasure
You relish my pain.
The harder you become
The more the sheets stain.
A little bump to help feel numb
To your every demand
The deeper I succumb.
Unable to escape
This torture's medieval.
Your games don't have a safe word,
You're fifty shades of evil.

The Cleansing

I bathe in the water.
The waves cleanse my soul.
Renewing my spirit,
Nature's baptism.

Little One

You feel just like sunshine
Warm upon my skin
And so brightly blinding.
Lightly scented as the sunflower,
Sweet as honeysuckle,
Soft as cotton tail
And as precious as a gem.

Still brand new as the dawn,
Yet deep as the ocean floor.
Joyful like a new love,
Fierce as a warrior.
You bring hope, love and faith
A new era to begin.

Heart Speech

You care too much.
You don't listen to me.
No matter how hard I beat this drum.
No matter how fiercely I break.
No matter if the flags are my color.
The very signal flows through your veins.
I cannot warn you any further
And still you persist,
Insist, you can't seem to resist
The hold on you.
I WILL cease to exist.
After all you can die
From a broken heart,
Don't say I didn't warn you.

Nothing But Fear

Don't let me stop you.
I will paralyze you in your tracks.
I will make you doubt.
You will question.
You will self sabotage.
Shake up your faith,
I am fear.

But you have control.
Be bold, be strong, be brave.
Cause baby no one's looking anyway.
This I promise.

I Am Woman.

Bathe in the power
Of your inner Goddess
Sit in your divine feminine energy
It's been gifted to you
This eternal power
Of the living portal
Connected otherworldly
Bound with our ancestors
Leading our daughters
Paving the way of empowerment
Strong sense of self
Honoring your worth
Fulfilling your journey
Liberating future generations

The Great Battle

Eyes wide open
You better be alert
Listen with your gut
Life by design
There is no coincidence
The change is slow
Little by little
The challenge real
Your will tested
You must be strong
You must have faith
You were created
In this exact time
To join the battle
You have the courage
Will you use it?
What shall be your choice?

(Can be read top to bottom or bottom to top and
it says nearly the same message.)

Mother Daughter Talk

You cannot go back
And change the past
Because you cannot
Take with you
The wisdom
Of the person you are now.

The Light In The Dark

I've been seeking a way out
Of this empty black abyss.
Much like a ship,
Lost at sea on a stormy night.
I am searching for the light in the dark.
And when that lights breaks through,
I shall embrace it and never let go.

The Photo

Flipping through an album
I found a picture of you.
That same familiar smile
Such a beautiful view.
I remember how you resisted,
Your hand up in protest.
Please don't take the photo,
I don't look my best.
And now I look at this picture,
A million memories in between.
And I'm thankful that I took it,
So I can see you more than in my dreams.

An Addicts Journey

I'm not here to play small
I'm here for the keeps
Take all that you have
Including your sleep
But that's just the start
You're in for a treat
How does it feel
To live on the streets
You lied and you stole
You cheated and bribed
Lost everything you know
Your daily life, to survive
Stuck in a cycle
You think, "I'm only 26"
You make the promises
Then go get your next fix

But in there somewhere
Is the person you were
Before life got hard
Before you felt so unsure
In you is someone
With so much light
You owe it to yourself
To win this fight

You're scared everyday
And yet you're still here
Sober is only
An unknown fear
You'll know when you're ready
A change comes from within
The path in you awakens
Suddenly you stand
Where once an addict had been

Up

But up

Else To go

Do not despair no where

When you are as you have

In the depths of hell

The Message

Today you sent me a message
In the form of a man
Who reminded me to be grateful
For all that I have and am
You do this quite often
To let me know you're there
Sometimes it's in a song
Sometimes a feeling in the air
I've learned overtime
To these messages I should listen
It's your way of telling me
To follow my intuition.

Just Let Go

Just let go
Be yourself
Unapologetically
Authentic
And proud of it
You get one chance
The time is now
Don't be afraid
Let them stare
Make them talk
In the end
They will wish
They just let go

Part Of Me

You will always be a part of me
You occupy a space
Deep within my being
That no one can replace
A piece of you on my mind
When I think of times together
A lot of you rests in my heart
There's so much we have wethered
A little bit of you appears
Especially when I smile
So much laughter we have shared
All across the miles
Mostly I find you in my soul
Our connection can't be broken
Thank you God for my sister
No other would I have chosen.